HOW DOES IT FLY?

GLIDER

BY NANCY ROBINSON MASTERS

CHERRY LAKE
Publishing

Published in the United States of America by Cherry Lake Publishing
Ann Arbor, Michigan
www.cherrylakepublishing.com

Content Adviser: Jacob Zeiger, Production Support Engineer, the Boeing Company

Photo Credits: Cover and page 1, ©iStockphoto.com/ArgestesArgestes; page 5, ©Judex/Shutterstock, Inc.; page 7, ©Graham Prentice/Shutterstock, Inc.; page 9, ©Boerescu/Shutterstock, Inc.; page 11, ©a123luha/Shutterstock, Inc.; page 13, ©Ellen Isaacs/Alamy; page 15, ©Bernhard Schiestel/Dreamstime.com; page 17, ©Zentilia/Dreamstime.com; page 19, ©imagebroker/Alamy; page 21, ©Sandyprints/Dreamstime.com.

LIBRARY OF CONGRESS CATALOGING-IN-PUBLICATION DATA
Masters, Nancy Robinson.
How does it fly? Glider/by Nancy Robinson Masters.
p. cm.—(Community connections)
Includes bibliographical references and index.
ISBN-13: 978-1-61080-072-3 (lib. bdg.)
ISBN-10: 1-61080-072-9 (lib. bdg.)
1. Gliders (Aeronautics)—Juvenile literature. 2. Gliding and soaring—Juvenile literature.
I. Title. II. Title: Glider.
TL761.M37 2011
629.133'33—dc22 2011000270

Cherry Lake Publishing would like to acknowledge the work of The Partnership for 21st Century Skills. Please visit *www.21stcenturyskills.org* for more information.

Printed in the United States of America
Corporate Graphics Inc.
July 2011
CLFA09

GLIDER

CONTENTS

KINDS OF GLIDERS

A glider is a kind of airplane. Most gliders do not have engines.

Gliders come in different sizes. Hang gliders look like big kites. Paragliders look like parachutes. Pilots ride under the hang glider or paraglider wing. They have to run on foot to take off.

Hang glider pilots often take off from high cliffs and mountains. This pilot looks like an insect in flight!

Sailplanes are gliders with very long wings. They look like small, thin airplanes. The pilot sits in a seat like an airplane pilot.

A **tow rope** hooks the sailplane to a **powered airplane**. The airplane drags the sailplane into the air. The sailplane pilot pulls a handle to unhook the tow rope. This lets the sailplane glide on its own.

This sailplane is being towed into the air by a small powered airplane.

THINK!

The space shuttle took off by using its engines. It did not use its engines when it landed. It landed as a glider. Why do you think the space shuttle landed as a glider?

RISING AIR

Gravity pulls the glider down. Lift pushes the glider up. Gliders must have lift to fly.

Rising air creates lift. **Updrafts** and **thermals** are kinds of rising air. Updrafts are found near hills and mountains. Wind is forced up when it hits a hill or mountain.

A paraglider catches an updraft near a mountainside.

Thermals are areas of heated air. Heated air rises. A thermal can rise very high very quickly.

Gliders gain **altitude** from updrafts and thermals. They **soar** into the air. They lose altitude away from updrafts and thermals. A glider stays in the sky by flying between updrafts and thermals.

Glider pilots use updrafts and thermals to stay in the air.

MAKE A GUESS!

How long do you think a glider can keep flying? Can you guess the longest time a glider has ever flown? The world record is about 1,900 miles (3,000 kilometers). It took 15 hours!

GLIDING SKILLS

Glider pilots find rising air. They watch for birds gliding in circles. These birds are often riding a thermal. High, tall clouds may be part of an updraft.

Glider pilots listen to the air moving around the glider. They listen for changes in the sound of the air.

Glider pilots must pay close attention to the air around them.

LOOK!

Look for signs of updrafts and thermals. One way to find them is to look for birds that are flying without flapping their wings. What other signs can you see?

Glider pilots use their hands and feet to move controls. The controls move parts of the wings and tail.

Spoilers are parts of the wings. They are like brakes. The pilot uses spoilers to lose altitude quickly.

A pilot pushes or pulls on a bar to control a hang glider.

Instruments help the pilot fly the glider. The **altimeter** shows the pilot how high the glider is. The **variometer** shows how fast the glider is going up or down.

Glider pilots learn to use each instrument in a sailplane.

CREATE!

Create a list of skills that are needed to fly gliders. How many of these skills do you have? How might you learn the other skills on your list?

BUILDING GLIDERS

Inventors such as Otto Lilienthal built the first gliders in the 1800s. They used gliders to test ideas and learn more about flying. Their gliders were made of wood covered in fabric.

Gliders are still built to test new ideas. Most gliders are built for **sport flying**.

Models of some of Lilienthal's gliders can be seen in museums.

Gliders today are often built of new materials called **composites**. Composites begin as a cloth of strong fibers. These fibers are hardened with thick, honey-like glue called resin. Composites are superstrong. They are very light.

Gliders built with composites can soar higher. They can fly faster. They can stay in the air longer.

New sailplanes are often made with carbon composite material.

MAKE A GUESS!

Think about what a glider needs in order to fly. Will gliders be used to explore other planets? Ask a teacher, librarian, or parent to help you find an answer. Did you guess correctly?

GLOSSARY

altimeter (al-TIM-uh-tur) instrument that shows how high the glider is above the ground

altitude (AL-tih-tood) distance above the ground

composites (kuhm-PAH-zitss) strong, lightweight materials made of fibers that are hardened into shape with resin

powered airplane (POW-urd AYR-playn) an airplane with an engine

soar (SOR) fly high on rising air

spoilers (SPOIL-urz) parts of a glider wing used to make the glider lose altitude quickly

sport flying (SPORT FLY-ing) flying for fun

thermals (THUR-muhlz) areas of heated air

tow rope (TOH-ROPE) a rope used to pull a sailplane off the ground

updrafts (UP-draftss) rising air

variometer (vayr-ee-AHM-uh-tur) instrument that shows how fast a glider is going up or down

FIND OUT MORE

BOOKS

Dewar, Andrew. *Simple Origami Airplanes*. North Clarendon, VT: Tuttle Publishing, 2010.

Hodgkins, Fran. *How People Learned to Fly*. New York: HarperCollins, 2007.

WEB SITES

NASA: Ultra-Efficient Engine Technology—Kid's Page
www.ueet.nasa.gov/StudentSite/
Find information about how planes fly and about the history of flight, play some games, and more.

Soaring Society of America
www.ssa.org/
Look at photos and videos, and find information about sailplanes.

INDEX

ABOUT THE AUTHOR

Nancy Robinson Masters is a pilot. She is the author of many books and stories. Flying is one of her favorite things to write about. Her husband, Bill, teaches people how to fly gliders. Bill and Nancy live at an airport near Abilene, Texas.